A TRUE BOOK™

Queens and Princesses

Grace
of Monaco

Michael Burgan

Children's Press®
An Imprint of Scholastic Inc.

Content Consultant
Mita Choudhury
Professor of History
Vassar College
Poughkeepsie, New York

Library of Congress Cataloging-in-Publication Data
Names: Burgan, Michael, author.
Title: Grace of Monaco / by Michael Burgan.
Description: [First edition]. |New York, NY : Children's Press, an imprint of Scholastic Inc., 2020. |
　　Series: A true book | Includes bibliographical references and index. | Audience: Grades 4–6. |
　　Summary: "The book explains the life of Princess Grace."—Provided by publisher.
Identifiers: LCCN 2019031687 | ISBN 9780531131732 (library binding) | ISBN 9780531134337 (paperback)
Subjects: LCSH: Grace, Princess of Monaco, 1929-1982—Juvenile literature. | Princesses—Monaco—
　　Biography—Juvenile literature. | Motion picture actors and actresses—United States—Biography—
　　Juvenile literature.
Classification: LCC DC943.G7 B87 2020 | DDC 944.9/49092 [B]—dc23

Book produced by 22 MEDIAWORKS, INC.
Book design by Amelia Leon / Fabia Wargin Design

Front cover: Grace Kelly in 1956
Back cover: A wedding portrait
of Prince Rainier and
Princess Grace of Monaco

Find the Truth

Everything you are about to read is true *except* for one of the sentences on this page.

Which one is **TRUE**?

T or F — Grace Kelly and Prince Rainier knew each other for many years before they married.

T or F — Princess Grace helped raise money for charities in Monaco.

Find the answers in this book.

Contents

Princess Grace and Prince Rainier

Grace Kelly starred in *To Catch a Thief* in 1955.

The BIG Truth

From America to Monaco

4 A Lasting Legacy

In 1956, Grace Kelly appeared in the movie *High Society*.

An American Princess

In 1955, **Grace Kelly was one of the most successful actresses in Hollywood.** Her **talent** and her **beauty** had propelled her to the heights of **fame**, despite her parent's disapproval of her chosen profession.

Then, one year later, everything changed. She married Prince Rainier and became Her Serene Highness, Princess Grace of Monaco. In her new role, Grace raised a family and worked to make Monaco a better place to live. Her **intelligence** and **independent nature** helped her succeed as an actress and as a princess.

During the 1920s, Grace's father, Jack, won three Olympic gold medals for rowing.

As a child, Grace (left) learned how to arrange flowers, and it remained a favorite hobby.

Life in America

Grace Patricia Kelly was born on November 12, 1929. Her grandfather had **immigrated** to the United States from Ireland in 1867 and built a successful construction company. His son, Jack (Grace's father), took over the company and soon became a millionaire. He built his family a large house in a wealthy Philadelphia neighborhood. Grace lived there with her parents, her older brother, John Jr., and her sisters, Margaret and Elizabeth. The family also spent time at their summer home in New Jersey. The Kelly family **embodied** the American dream.

Grace

The Kelly family lived in a brick mansion with 17 rooms and its own tennis court.

A Young Actress

Grace was a quiet girl and spent much of her time at home reading or playing with dolls. At 11, she appeared in her first play, called *Don't Feed the Animals*. She already seemed to have a **flair** for acting.

In high school, Grace was well liked and loved to laugh. After graduation, she moved to New York City to study acting.

Going to Hollywood

It didn't take Grace long to find success. By 1950, she had appeared on TV and in a Broadway play. Grace was just 20 years old.

Grace soon moved to Hollywood, California, to find work in films. The first movie she appeared in was called *Fourteen Hours*. She was on-screen for only two minutes!

In *To Catch a Thief*, Grace played a rich woman who falls in love with a jewel thief.

A Rising Star

Grace's next movie was a western called *High Noon*. Her co-star in the film was Gary Cooper, a famous actor at the time. His popularity meant many people would see the film—and Grace in it. Released in 1952, *High Noon* won several Academy Awards (known as "Oscars").

Through 1952, Grace made movies for MGM, a major film **studio**. She also began working with Alfred Hitchcock, a famous Hollywood **director**.

In *High Society*, Grace sang a song with co-star Bing Crosby, shown here on the left.

Grace in a scene from a movie called *Rear Window*, directed by Alfred Hitchcock.

Grace Kelly appeared twice on the cover of *Life* magazine: in 1954 and 1955.

Grace Takes Home an Award

Grace was one of the hardest-working actresses in Hollywood. During a period of about 14 months, she made six films. One of them was *The Country Girl*, which came out in 1954. In many of her earlier roles, she had looked glamorous. For this movie, she played a housewife who wore simple dresses. She won an Academy Award for Best Actress for *The Country Girl*.

The Grimaldi family have ruled Monaco for 700 years.

Monaco is just a few miles away from Italy. It is smaller than Central Park in New York City.

Meeting Her Prince

In May 1955, Grace Kelly went to a film festival in Cannes, France. On the trip, she visited the tiny **principality** of Monaco. Located on the Mediterranean Sea, Monaco was famous for its casino in a district called Monte Carlo. For decades, wealthy Europeans visited Monaco to gamble and spend time at the beach. On her trip, Grace briefly met Monaco's ruler, Prince Rainier Grimaldi.

Who Was Prince Rainier?

The prince's full name was Rainier Louis Henri Maxence Bertrand de Grimaldi. He had **ascended** to the throne in 1949, becoming Prince Rainier III.

When he met Grace, Rainier was 32, and he was looking for a princess. By law, he needed to marry and have a child. Otherwise, France would take control of Monaco. His people were eager for him to find a wife so France would not rule the principality again. But Rainier did not want to marry just to obey the law. He wanted to find a wife that he deeply loved.

Prince Rainier went to schools in England and learned to speak English well.

In the movie *The Swan*, Grace played a princess looking for a marriage proposal.

Thinking of Marriage

A few months after her trip to Europe, Grace starred in her next movie, *The Swan*. But Grace was restless. Living and working in Hollywood wasn't enough for her anymore. During the summer of 1955, Grace attended her sister's wedding. She began to think it was time to get married and have children.

The Prince Takes Action

After their meeting in Monaco, Grace and Rainier became pen pals and friends. Grace learned that she and Rainier shared strong religious beliefs. They also had a similar sense of humor. With each letter, the two told each other more and more about themselves. They soon realized they loved each other.

In December 1955, Rainier met Grace in New York. He asked her to marry him, and Grace said yes.

Prince Rainier was late for his first meeting with Grace. She wore this dress that day.

Grace and Prince Rainier saw each other less than five times before they married.

Engaged!

The couple soon announced to the world their plans to marry. The news brought rejoicing in Monaco, where the people waved U.S. flags along with their own. Grace said that she planned to finish her contract with MGM. She still enjoyed acting. But as she said years later, she didn't like all the attention she got as a movie star.

Grace's engagement ring was a 10-carat emerald cut stone from the world-famous jeweler, Cartier.

Grace met reporters before leaving for Monaco. She took her dog with her on the trip.

Sailing to Monaco

Still, Grace had one more film to make, *High Society*, a movie musical. Before her departure for Monaco, she met with about 200 reporters who shouted questions at her. True to her nature, Grace remained calm, despite the chaos of the event. Then, in April 1956, Grace and 80 friends and relatives sailed to Monaco on the S.S. *Constitution*.

The Royal Way

Royal families often exchanged money as they arranged weddings between their children. The parents of the bride usually paid money called a **dowry** to the groom's family. When Grace Kelly was planning her wedding, Prince Rainier asked her father to pay a dowry, reported to be $2 million! Some people think Grace paid it herself.

Grace's wedding dress was a gift from MGM Studios.

The Big Day—Times Two!

Across the world, people waited for what was being called "the wedding of the century." More than 1,600 reporters and photographers flocked to Monaco for the event. It lasted two days. On April 18, 1956 Grace and Rainier were married in the prince's palace. The wedding was a **civil** ceremony, which made the marriage official under Monaco's

The people of Monaco presented Princess Grace with a white dove to celebrate her marriage to Prince Rainier.

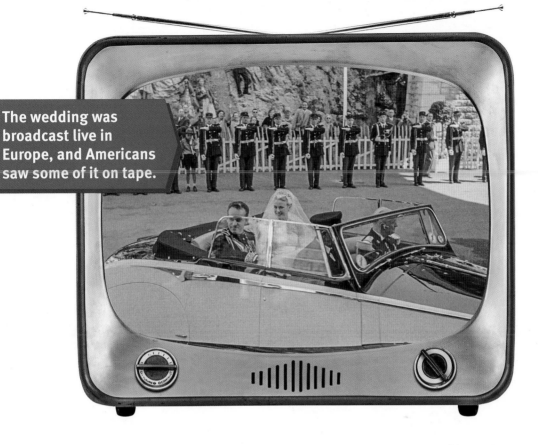

The wedding was broadcast live in Europe, and Americans saw some of it on tape.

The next day, Grace and Rainier were married again in a Roman Catholic church. Six hundred people attended the ceremony, including some of Grace's Hollywood friends, such as film star Cary Grant. When the wedding was over, Grace Kelly was officially Her Serene Highness, Princess Grace of Monaco. She and her prince then attended a grand party.

Monaco's official language is French. Soon after she was married, Grace began learning it so she could speak with the people there.

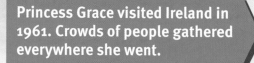

Princess Grace visited Ireland in 1961. Crowds of people gathered everywhere she went.

The Life of a Princess

Becoming a princess was not easy for Grace. She had to convince the **Monegasques,** the people of Monaco, that she was fit to be a princess. Rainier needed to improve Monaco's economy so people had good jobs and places to live. Could an actress help lead the country? Grace also had to win over Rainier's family, who did not know her very well. Few believed she would be successful in her role.

Life in a Palace

Grace also had to adjust to living in a centuries-old palace with more than 100 rooms! Many of them were filled with fine furniture and valuable pieces of art.

About 250 people worked there, including cooks, housekeepers, groundskeepers, and guards. It was difficult to be around so many strangers and she often felt alone.

Grace and her new family lived in just a small part of Monaco's huge palace.

Princess Grace and Prince Rainier wave to crowds outside the palace in Monaco after the baptism of their first child, Caroline.

Becoming a Mother

In 1957, Grace's life changed again as she became a mother. She and Rainier had a daughter they named Caroline. The next year, they had a son named Albert. In 1965, they had their third child, Stephanie. Grace enjoyed being a mother. But her duties as a princess made it hard for her to spend as much time with her children as she would have liked.

Sometimes Grace would allow Caroline and Albert to help her choose what clothes she would wear.

Working for the People of Monaco

As a princess, Grace helped with several charities. One of them was the Monaco Red Cross. Like other Red Cross organizations, it provides aid to people in need and promotes good health. Grace's fame drew many wealthy supporters from around the world. She also worked closely with Rainier as he tried to improve Monaco.

In 1956, Grace and Rainier gave money to the March of Dimes, a charity that supports health care for mothers and children.

For many years Monaco had relied on its casino for most of its money. Grace helped make people more aware of the country's beauty. She invited well-known performers to Monaco, thus increasing the number of tourists who visited. Rainier was able to bring in new business and create more jobs.

Grace also spent time with the sick and elderly. She knew all the hospital patients by their first names.

Grace raised money to build a day-care center for the children of working mothers.

Grace's efforts to help children in need led the people to love and respect her.

Relaxing in the Country

As the years passed, Grace found time to set aside her duties as princess and enjoy her life. During the summers, she and Rainier brought their family to their summer home, called Roc Agel. It sat just over the border in France. There, she liked to cook and arrange flowers. The prince planted gardens and took care of a small farm.

The family's summer home, Roc Agel, has 125 acres and sits on a mountain called Mont Agel.

In 1978, Grace read poetry on stage in Pittsburgh, Pennsylvania, in a show called *Birds, Beasts, and Flowers*.

Still a Performer

In 1962, Alfred Hitchcock wanted Grace to star in a movie he was making called *Marnie*. She turned him down, but still had an interest in making movies. During the 1960s, she made two **documentaries** about Monaco. In these short films, she told viewers about her new home. Finally, in 1976, she performed in front of a live audience for the first time since she had acted in plays more than two decades before.

From America to Monaco

When Grace became Her Serene Highness, Princess Grace of Monaco, she had to make many changes to her life. Some of them were not easy!

Grace stars in *To Catch a Thief*.

At Work

In America, Grace was a successful actress who earned her own money and lived independently.

In Monaco, Grace gave up her acting career to pursue the duties and charitable work required of a princess.

Grace and her mother.

Friends and Family

In America, Grace always had friends close by whether she was working in New York or Hollywood. She could easily visit her family, too.

In Monaco, Grace found herself missing people from her former life. She eagerly awaited calls from friends in the United States.

A New Role

In America, Grace went on dates, but she never married or had any children.

In Monaco, Grace learned to juggle her official duties with being a wife, and a mother to her three children.

Grace with Albert and Caroline.

In 1982, Princess Grace approved the script for a television movie about her life.

An exhibition in Paris in 2008, dedicated to the memory of Princess Grace, featured many of the magazine covers she appeared on through the years.

A Lasting Legacy

Americans never seemed to grow tired of reading about Grace Kelly. Over the years, she was interviewed by many magazines. As a princess, she met many famous people, such as U.S. president Ronald Reagan and first lady Nancy Reagan. She represented her adopted country of Monaco with dignity.

When Grace met Diana Spencer in 1981, she told Diana it was not easy being a princess.

Another "Wedding of the Century"

The famous people Grace knew included Prince Charles of Britain. When he married Diana Spencer in July 1981, the couple asked Grace and Rainier to walk ahead of all the royalty who attended. Grace had met Diana before and they got along well. Diana felt she had something in common with Grace, since they both married into ruling families.

A Tragic End

Grace may have wanted to return to acting, but she never got the chance. On September 13, 1982, she was driving with her daughter Stephanie on the hilly, curvy roads outside Monaco. Grace lost control of the car and it fell down a hillside. Both she and Stephanie were hurt, but Grace did not survive her injuries. She died the next day.

A memorial for Grace (top) sits near the site where her car crashed.

The World Mourns

The news of Grace's death at the young age of 52 stunned the world. Rainier wept openly for his wife. Royalty from across Europe, including Princess Diana, came to her funeral service. First lady Nancy Reagan came too, as did many of Grace's Hollywood friends. The service for Grace was broadcast on television, and as many as 100 million people watched it.

A legacy is something that people leave behind after they die. It can be something solid, like money or jewels. Or it can be memories of all they did while they were alive. Grace left behind a lasting legacy based on all she did. People remembered her talent as an actress. They admired how she adjusted to her new life as a princess. And she was known for all the good work she had done for charities.

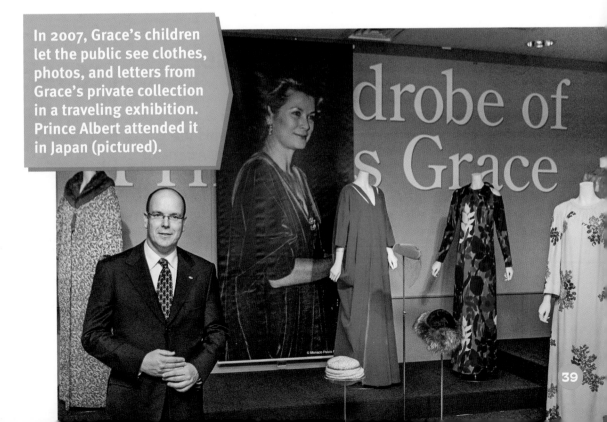

In 2007, Grace's children let the public see clothes, photos, and letters from Grace's private collection in a traveling exhibition. Prince Albert attended it in Japan (pictured).

Giving Back

Prince Rainier helped keep Grace's legacy alive by starting the Princess Grace Foundation—USA shortly after her death. It gives money to artists around the world. In 2017, Prince Albert bought the house in Philadelphia where his mother grew up. He plans to move some of the foundation's offices into the home.

Timeline of Princess Grace

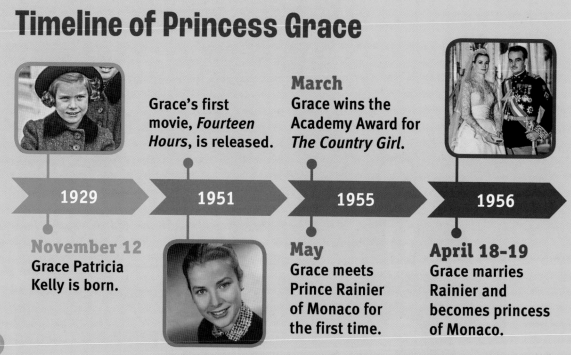

Grace's first movie, *Fourteen Hours*, is released.

March
Grace wins the Academy Award for *The Country Girl*.

1929 **1951** **1955** **1956**

November 12
Grace Patricia Kelly is born.

May
Grace meets Prince Rainier of Monaco for the first time.

April 18-19
Grace marries Rainier and becomes princess of Monaco.

The interest in Grace and her family lives on. Prince Albert and his sisters sometimes give interviews about their mother, and their own lives are often featured in the media. In 2017, Albert gave a tour of the Grimaldi palace in Monaco to a U.S. television network.

Time has passed, but Grace remains one of the most famous princesses of modern times.

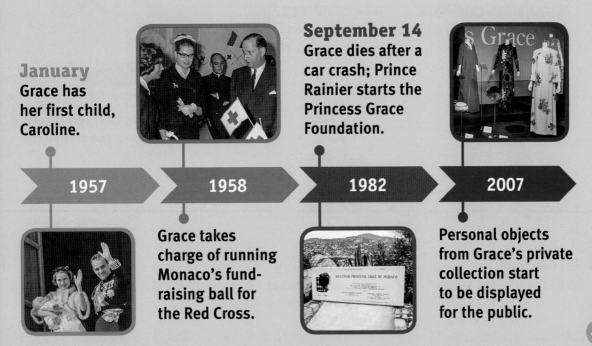

January
Grace has her first child, Caroline.

September 14
Grace dies after a car crash; Prince Rainier starts the Princess Grace Foundation.

1957

1958

1982

2007

Grace takes charge of running Monaco's fund-raising ball for the Red Cross.

Personal objects from Grace's private collection start to be displayed for the public.

Grace's Family Tree

John "Jack" Kelly Sr. was an Olympic rower.

1899–1960

Margaret Majer married Jack Kelly in 1924.

1898–1990

Margaret "Peggy" Kelly was her father's favorite child.

1925–1991

John "Kell" Kelly Jr. was a star rower, just like his father.

1927–1985

Grace Kelly is best remembered as Princess Grace of Monaco.

1929–1982

Princess Caroline of Hanover helps support the charities her mother founded.

1957–

Prince Albert II succeeded his father as Monaco's ruler in 2005.

1958–

Prince Pierre, Duke of Valentinois, was born in France.

Princess Charlotte, Duchess of Valentinois, was a Grimaldi.

Elizabeth "Lizanne" Kelly sometimes lived with Grace in Hollywood.

Prince Rainier III won a medal for his bravery during World War II.

Princess Antoinette, Baroness of Massy, was president of Monaco's Society for the Protection of Animals.

Princess Stephanie of Monaco does work for AIDS charities.

LEGEND

 The pink gem and dark green branches show each marriage.

The light green branches show the children of each marriage.

An orange frame indicates male.

A purple frame indicates female.

43

Number of live TV shows Grace Kelly appeared in: More than 30

Number of Hollywood films Grace Kelly made before she married Prince Rainier: 11

Population of Monaco in 2019: Just over 37,000 people

Percentage of Monegasques who are foreign-born as of 2019: 75

Length of Prince Rainier's rule at his death in 2005: 56 years—longer than any other European ruler at that time

Cost of tickets for the Monaco Red Cross Ball in 2020: About $3,800

Number of artists who took part in a 2019 exhibit to mark the 90th year of Grace's birth: 50

Did you find the truth?

F Grace Kelly and Prince Rainier knew each other for many years before they married.

T Princess Grace helped raise money for charities in Monaco.

Resources

Further Reading

King, David C. *Monaco*. New York: Marshall Cavendish Benchmark, 2008.

Norwich, Grace. *The Real Princess Diaries*. New York: Scholastic, 2015.

O'Shei, Tim. *Princess Grace of Monaco*. Mankato, MN: Capstone Press, 2009.

Pollack, Pam, and Meg Belviso. *Who Was Alfred Hitchcock?* New York: Grosset & Dunlap, 2014.

Rauf, Don. *Hollywood*. Ann Arbor, MI: Cherry Lake Publishing, 2017.

Taraborrelli, J. Randy. *Once Upon a Time: Behind the Fairy Tale of Princess Grace and Prince Rainier*. New York: Rose Books, 2003.

Other Books in the Series

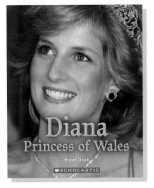

Glossary

ascended (uh-SEND-ed) moved up

civil (SI-vuhl) of or having to do with the laws of a country

director (duh-REK-tur) someone who directs a play or movie

documentaries (dahk-yuh-MEN-tur-eez) movies or television programs about real people or events

dowry (DOU-ree) money or property that a woman's family supplies to a man in some cultures when the woman marries him

embodied (em-BAH-deed) gave a solid form to an idea or feeling

flair (flair) a natural ability or skill

immigrated (IM-i-gray-ted) moved from one country to another in order to settle there

Monegasques (MON-eh-gasks) the people of Monaco

principality (prin-suh-PAL-it-ee) a country ruled by a prince

studio (STOO-dee-oh) a place where movies, television and radio shows, or recordings are made

Index

Page numbers in **bold** indicate illustrations.

About the Author

Over the past 25 years, Michael Burgan has written more than 250 books for children and teens. His favorite subjects are U.S. history and biographies of famous people. To write this book, he used many articles from newspapers and magazines written during and after Grace Kelly's life. He is a big fan of the movies she made with Alfred Hitchcock. Michael studied history at the University of Connecticut. He currently lives in Santa Fe, New Mexico, and he's written a True Book about that state.